AF148813

Princess Diana Speaks from Heaven:

A Divine Revelation

Matthew Robert Payne

This book is copyrighted by Matthew Robert Payne. Copyright © 2017. All rights reserved.

No part of this publication may be reproduced, stored in a retrieval system, or transmitted in any way by any means, electronic, mechanical, photocopy, recording, or otherwise, without the prior permission of the author except as provided by USA copyright law.

Please visit http://personal-prophecy-today.com to sow into Matthew's writing ministry, to request a personal prophecy or life coaching, or to contact him.

Cover designed by akira007 at fiverr.com.

Edited by Lisa Thompson at www.writebylisa.com You can email Lisa at writebylisa@gmail.com for your editing needs.

All Scripture is taken from the New King James Version® unless otherwise indicated. Copyright © 1982 by Thomas Nelson. Used by permission. All rights reserved.

The opinions expressed by the author are not necessarily those of Revival Waves of Glory Books & Publishing.

Published by Revival Waves of Glory Books & Publishing PO Box 596| Litchfield, Illinois 62056 USA

Revival Waves of Glory Books & Publishing is committed to excellence in the publishing industry. Their website is www.revivalwavesofgloryministries.com Book design Copyright © 2017 by Revival Waves of Glory Books & Publishing. All rights reserved.

Paperback:

Hardcover:

Dedication

I want to dedicate this book to all the people who are hungry for more of God. Some of us are not satisfied with being "normal" or "content" or with simply coasting along in life. Some of us want the "more" and are open to new things. If you are one of these people, I dedicate this book to you.

Acknowledgements

Father God

I want to thank you for loving me, for leading me, and for making me into the person that I am today. Thank you for your Son, my best friend. Thank you for your Holy Spirit and Jesus. I thank you for allowing me to have supernatural experiences with people like Diana.

Jesus Christ

Thank you for being my friend for all of my life. I cannot thank you enough for all that you do in my life. I live to serve you and to do everything that you call me to do. I cannot imagine life without you. I thank you and the Holy Spirit each day for guiding me. I want to thank you for introducing me to Diana and allowing her to become close to me.

Bill Vincent

I want to thank Bill Vincent, who produces my paperback books, my e-books, and my audio books. His company, Revival Waves of Glory Books & Publishing, has shown me great favor, and without him, I would be spending a lot more money to produce books. I give him my heartfelt thanks.

Jeff

I want to thank Jeff for his thoughtful donation to fully fund this book. Jeff's heavenly bank account will be credited with this reward.

The Readers

I want to thank my readers. I hope that you enjoy this book, and I hope that it encourages you to become a more devoted follower of Jesus. I encourage you to press on to become everything that you can possibly be.

Ministry Supporters

I want to thank all the people who have requested a prophecy from me, those who have requested a life-coaching session, and those who have requested your own message from an angel. I want to thank all those who have sown into my book-writing ministry, like Jeff who I mentioned above. Without you, this book would not have been possible. I am so happy for you.

June and Bob Payne

I want to thank my mother and father for all of their love and support.

Friends

I want to thank friends like Lisa, Lance, David, Michael, Wendy, Suzie, Mary, and more for loving and accepting me.

Table of Contents

Question 1:

How do you like being here today?

The ability to come down here and speak to the people is a fascinating concept. I had no idea that I was going to be given the opportunity to come and speak.

When I first arrived in heaven, I needed to adjust to the lifestyle here. A short time later, I was told about Matthew and how I was going to interact with him and spend some time with him. I was told that in the future, he was going to interview me and that he was going to self-publish a book and make it available for people to read.

Matthew's a small-time person. He is not a big name or a well-known personality in the world, so his books aren't bestsellers on the *New York Times* list. However, some Christians and others who are interested in hearing what I have to say will find this book.

I'm humbled to be given the opportunity to come to earth and say a few things. Of course, the Lord might make it possible for me to have a bigger voice and a bigger opportunity to speak through someone who will be able to take my message to the whole world, but I'm very glad to be here today.

Some people will get to meet me. Jesus will open up the opportunity for some people to meet me and interact with me.

I've learned a lot since I've been in heaven, and I have a lot to offer. The culture of heaven really refines you and makes you concentrate on what's redeemable, what's important, and what's worthwhile in your personality and in your life. Strip away the carnal thoughts and what you think about my marriage and its breakdown and even about the suspicious circumstances surrounding my death. Earthly things pass away when you are in heaven. The culture of heaven seems to take over and make everything beautiful.

The Lord Jesus redeems things. He takes what was bad, what had a tarnished reputation, and even what was partially okay, and he polishes them and recreates situations, upgrading you in such a way that everything about you is beautiful and fully restored into its greatest glory.

With that being said, I won't spend a lot of time in this interview talking about earthly things or about my past life that I lived and how I felt. I will spend some of my time here answering questions and talking about my life and what I'm experiencing right now. I'll speak about the hope of heaven and the ability for people to come here and to live an extraordinary and totally fantastic life. I hope that over the course of this interview, you come to realize that it really is me, Princess Diana, the former princess of Wales, speaking to you. It is my pleasure to be here and spend the time answering these questions.

Let me assure you that I am happy to be here and overjoyed to be counted worthy by Jesus Christ to come and speak to all of you. Not everyone has the opportunity to come back from the dead as it were with something to say that will impact those living on earth.

Question 2:

How did we meet?

The first time that I met Matthew was when he was watching a YouTube video of Prince William, my son, marrying Kate. This was quite a number of years ago, and Matthew was in his bedroom with his computer. However, his computer hasn't been in his bedroom for years.

He was enjoying watching Kate marry Prince William. I came alongside him and watched the wedding with him and was commenting on the ceremony as it progressed. Matthew wasn't aware that I was in heaven up until that point and was surprised and happy to see me.

Once again, like when Matthew met Michael Jackson, he was surprised that he was able to meet someone who had been so popular on earth when they were living. Sometimes, it takes Matthew by surprise to meet people who have a very big reputation on earth with the ability to change and affect people's lives. Together, we watched the video on YouTube of the wedding, and I was able to converse with Matthew and talk to him about my love for William and my happiness with all the details of the wedding, the procession, the dress, and different details.

Matthew does not understand fabric and fashion, so I can't really use his voice here to describe what I thought of the dress, but I was very pleased with how Kate looked. I was very happy that my son had found love in such a dimension that he committed his life to her, a woman who would continue to become a new queen of the empire if everything goes as planned. I was very emotional and in a really good frame of mind to be watching it.

Of course, I was able to watch the wedding from heaven. I didn't necessarily need to come to earth to watch the wedding through YouTube on Matthew's computer. However, Jesus Christ allowed it and arranged for it to happen so that Matthew might have the first opportunity to meet me and to know that I'm alive and in heaven. I have been selected to interact with his life and be one of the people with whom he interacts.

He was once watching a documentary of Steve Jobs' life and was interested in it. He had read the biography of Steve Jobs and wanted to learn as much he could about him. As he was watching a documentary on YouTube, Steve Jobs appeared to him. As is often the case with Matthew, if he's talking to someone about a departed saint or watching a YouTube video about the person, that saint commonly appears and spiritually materializes in front of Matthew.

This wasn't out of the ordinary for Matthew. Of course, he was surprised and amazed, but he could handle it. Another time when I came to earth, Jesus spoke to Matthew as he was walking down to his gas station. Matthew has a lot of encounters with the supernatural as he walks down to his gas station. His brain is at rest during this time, and his mind isn't active or busy on Facebook or doing something with his computer.

As he was walking down to the gas station, Jesus asked if Matthew would be able to write a letter from me to Prince William, and Matthew agreed. Then, I appeared, walking next to him, and I was overjoyed. I asked him if he was really going to write a letter for me, and he confirmed that he was. We went to the gas station, and he bought some milk. I went back to his place.

He found the official address to send letters to Prince William, opened up his Microsoft Word, and typed out a letter that I dictated to William. Then, he sent it off to William. Although he didn't receive a reply, he assumed that the palace probably passed it on to William.

I have met Matthew on a number of occasions. Recently, I've come into his life and have interacted and spent time with him going out. I go shopping and walking with him, discussing his life and directing him in some ways, keeping him company. I have a purpose in his life that will continue in the future. That's how we met and how we know each other. Much of the reason that we met and spent time together was to give Matthew a sense of comfort with me so that when he was called upon to interview me that he'd be quite happy and relaxed to sit down and listen to my words and dictate what I have to say so that we could make it into a book.

Question 3:

What do you like about heaven?

Matthew has included this question in his first book with the interview with saints in _Great Cloud of Witnesses Speak_. He also asked Michael Jackson this same question in _Michael Jackson Speaks from Heaven: A Divine Revelation_. He also asked the question of people in _Great Cloud of Witnesses Speak: Old and New_, and they answered the question as well. One of the reasons for this question is that people are often fascinated with what heaven is like and excited to hear what those interviewed like about heaven.

The first thing that I want to mention about heaven that I enjoy is similar to what Mary Magdalene said in her interview, _Mary Magdalene Speaks from Heaven: A Divine Revelation._ I love the pageantry of heaven. Matthew has heard from people that in America, everything is done in a big way with a lot of pageantry and a lot of work that goes into productions. People are constantly trying to impress each other with how they celebrate and how they do things.

Nothing can be compared to heaven: the makeup, the gowns, the jewelry, the shoes. You will especially love heaven if any of the following apply to you:

- If you're a woman who likes beautiful, long, flowing gowns
- If you enjoy seeing beautiful diamonds and different gem stones displayed on women
- If you enjoy the best brands of shoes, and
- If you enjoy seeing women with wonderful figures.

I also love the fact that there's no fat in heaven. Fat doesn't exist. You have a perfect body, and everyone's face shines. Their faces shine according to the works that they did on earth. Their faces shine from different levels of glory, but from even the lowest amount of glory to the highest, people's faces shine. Their skin is radiant and beautiful, and people have perfect bodies.

Every person has a body that complements what their perfect appearance should have been on earth. For example, a teen girl with a great body might have the same body shape at an older age in heaven.

Heaven has incredible celebrations with amazing pageantry. In heaven, some fashion designers are as good as or better than those on earth. However, the difference between heaven and earth is that you can still obtain the gowns and dresses from reputable fashion designers in heaven even if you're not a model, a princess, or a movie star. If you're just an ordinary person, you can still obtain the amazing clothes.

You might think that my descriptions of things in heaven and what I enjoy there are really carnal. You might think that I'm not very spiritual because I speak of earthly things. Heaven is not just about spiritual things but caters to every dimension of your happiness. Please indulge me as I talk about something that made me happy on earth and that makes me even happier in heaven.

If you enjoy fashion, which I do, you can always be dressed in your best. You can always be looking your finest. You might shop for a dress or a gown just for one night. You can return it to the fashion designer at the end of the night. Someone else might pick it up, or it might just be used once for that occasion. You might keep it in your own bedroom or in a separate room for your clothes.

I have a separate room for my clothes with racks and racks of clothes that I hang up, prepared for me to wear. Imelda Marcos had hundreds of pairs of shoes, and when her kingdom went down, everyone was shocked to find out that she had two hundred pairs of shoes. I have to confess that I love my shoes, and I agree that a woman can never have too many pairs of shoes. This cliché is popular for a reason. That's one aspect of heaven that I really like.

I really enjoy the fashions, clothes, belts, ties, scarves, handbags, and accessories in heaven. I enjoy the jewelry, gemstones, diamonds, chains, necklaces, broaches, and all the accessories to what you're wearing. In heaven, you can afford anything you want, and I'll go into more detail on that later in the book.

Everyone in the world from the poor to the rich can dress really well in heaven. They can have all of the following:

- The very best of what's available in heaven
- Perfect dress with an outfit for every occasion
- The best-looking body
- Hair in the nicest fashion
- Immaculate grooming with the best nails and luminous skin, and
- Always looking your very best.

Of course, many women in heaven are from Africa or other poor nations of the world. They have no idea about some of the fashions available to women in the world. They might need to be schooled in fashion and learn about it and about what's beautiful. You can take lessons in fashion in heaven in order to learn what to wear, how to accessorize, and how to dress your very best. You can learn how to do that.

Of course, you can continue those fashion lessons and even go on to become a fashion designer in heaven. They can teach you the fine art of presenting clothes, creating designs, and making fashion so that other women in heaven can have beautiful clothes as well.

Another dimension of heaven is that everything is free. Everyone in heaven has a specific job, a job that was designed for them to do, a job that they love to do. They work those jobs in heaven for a certain amount of time per week in earthly terms. Heaven has different dimensions of time, but I will speak to you in earth terms.

People spend a certain amount of time at their jobs each week in heaven, but no one is paid to work. You don't derive an income from your job. You just do your job or career for enjoyment, and you will work at something that you enjoy. However, everything and everywhere in heaven—the clothes, the houses, the cars, the bicycles, the skateboards, the cafes, the restaurants, the books, the movies, the amusement parks, the entertainment—is free.

It's really true that you can take the dress back to the fashion designer after you're worn it for a night. A fashion designer might create a dress for you to wear for just one night. The extravagance of heaven is just amazing.

If things were free, how would you change? How would you eat if everything was free? Would you continue to eat at home in your kitchen each night, or would you eat out at a restaurant each night? Would you have a private catering firm come and cater parties and functions at your house? You have all these possible options. You can have a gourmet kitchen in your home so that you can create amazing food for yourself, your family, and your friends. You can have professional caterers come to your house and put on a party and cater the whole event. You can book a restaurant and have a party there, or you can have an intimate night out at a restaurant with someone that you love so that just the two of you spend time together eating dinner.

Many people wonder about relationships in heaven. Of course, a husband and wife who were married on earth will not be married to each other in heaven. In heaven, everyone has a relationship like brother and sister. The husband and wife will know their former partner, but they'll be like a brother and sister with a close relationship. There is no marriage or exclusivity in heaven. Heaven has no population growth except the growth from earth. No one has sex or babies. Heaven is only expanding from the population from earth. When I talk about an intimate dinner at a restaurant, it has no connotations of a sexual relationship. Instead, it is a private time with a friend for whom you have an intimate love. Two women can have an intimate dinner together because they are very close friends. They can have a beautiful dinner together and enjoy each other's company over fine food.

I enjoy the food and the restaurants in heaven. I enjoy the fact that I can have the very best of everything to my heart's desire and to my heart's content. When everything is free, this actually has a reverse effect on selfishness. When everything is available to you, you don't crave the very best for yourself like you do on earth where things cost money.

Here is another thing I like about heaven that is hard to comprehend for people who are living on earth. Economics is simply defined as "the allocation of scarce resources."[1] However, in heaven, there are no scarce resources. That's a hard concept with which to come to grips.

Heaven has no scarcity of excellent food, exquisite dresses, beautiful diamonds, and great gemstones. Heaven has no scarcity of beautiful houses, lush landscaping, fine restaurants, and wonderful parks and villages.

Heaven has no scarcity. An artist in heaven can paint a landscape, creating the landscape as they paint. Heaven is always expanding and getting bigger.

This concept is hard to explain and to share with people. There's no reason to be selfish in heaven because you can have

---

[1] Tim Worstall. 2016. "Economics Is Scarce Resources Allocation - What Resource Constraint Does Urban Farming Solve?" *Forbes,* August 4. Accessed August 28, 2017.
https://www.forbes.com/sites/timworstall/2016/08/15/economics-is-scarce-resources-allocation-what-resource-constraint-does-urban-farming-solve/#6e29c072a553.

whatever you like. You can dress in different clothes every single day, depending on what you do.

You can wear three pairs of shoes a day or even more, depending on the functions and the events that you attend. I enjoy going out in nature: parks, waterfalls, forests, and the natural beauty of heaven. I enjoy getting away from people and spending time by myself. I enjoy time with children. Many children are in heaven. Every child who never had the opportunity to accept Jesus in their life goes to heaven.

Of course, if you're an adult, you need to give your life to Jesus or accept him in your life to enter heaven. Jesus said in John 14:6, "I am the way, the truth and the life. No one comes to the Father except through me."

The entrance to heaven is through Jesus. However, children who were aborted had no chance to choose Jesus in their lives, so they all end up in heaven. I enjoy spending time with children in heaven, but I really enjoy spending time alone as well. As strange as it seems to many who will have read all the biographies and books about me, I really enjoy time alone. I enjoy getting away.

I've been involved in many things in heaven. I've had a role that's similar to a princess or a queen on earth where I've been at building dedications and been a part of official ceremonies. I've done many other things in heaven.

What else do I like about heaven? I love the fact that people in heaven do not have a carnal nature. Instead, they have a beautiful personality that's the very best that it can be. There's no envy, jealousy, selfishness, greed, anger, or malicious nature in heaven. There are no negative aspects to anyone's personality in heaven.

If Hitler, Stalin, or anyone else that you consider evil made it to heaven, all the best parts of their personalities would shine. I just used them as examples, but everyone who comes to heaven is transformed, and only the very best of who they are remains.

When you are dealing with people, you are connecting with the very best person that they can be. On earth, people really looked up to me, almost like a star. Even Matthew's mother watched documentaries about my life commemorating the twenty-year anniversary of my death. On earth, I couldn't just be an ordinary girl walking down the street. People flocked to me like they did to Michael Jackson.

I couldn't just live a private life as myself, but in heaven, people know who you are. No negative emotions—envy, greed, or jealousy—exist. No one looks at you as if you're some sort of star.

None of that is in heaven. Different people have different types of glory and are respected in various ways. The Apostle Paul is highly revered as are Moses and David. Although they are highly respected, they aren't worshipped as superstars the way that people are on earth. On earth, an ordinary person who is suddenly thrust into the spotlight can't live a normal life or go out and eat at a restaurant without paparazzi following, taking pictures, and making a big deal of everything.

What I really love about heaven is that I can walk down the street. I can go to a restaurant. I can go out in public, and people don't flock around me. No cameras flash. I'm not a superstar in heaven. I really love that. I have a chance to get to know myself and my best qualities. I can really shine and become the very best person that I can be.

What I love about heaven is that everyone is an individual. Earth is amazing, but only a small percentage of people on earth really find out what they're there to do. Many people are forced into earning an income and feel pressured to earn money to pay for their house, cars, clothes, and everything that they own.

Earth has such pressure to perform and make a living. In heaven, you have no financial pressure, no house to pay off, no car to pay for, no bills, and no expenses. You don't have to pay electricity, light bills, or gas bills. You don't have to slave away each week just to earn money to live.

Since the pressure is off and since heaven has all the information in the universe, you can find out what you're created to do and what your purpose is. On earth as a Christian, you can consult a prophet and ask him or her about two or three things that you feel led to do in your life. You can ask which one God would prefer you to do.

A prophet might choose one and be accurate and direct you. However, many people on earth never find out what they were born to do. In heaven, it's different. Everyone is an individual, but they all know why they're there and what they're born to do.

Many people in heaven get to do what they're created to do on earth, but they never had the opportunity to do. Some people are really gifted in administration, paperwork, shuffling files, processing information, and keeping an organization running. They can do that in heaven and do an extraordinary job. Some people are a bit of a character, and they might have really enjoyed acting. Perhaps they'd had roles in a few plays or movies on earth. In heaven, they become an actor and spend much of their time acting in new films that are released there. Everyone in heaven watches movies according to their personal tastes.

Actors appear in one film after another, starring in roles and really loving what they do. On earth, you might want to counsel and guide as a life coach. In heaven, you might become a heavenly mentor who directs others into their best lives.

Whoever you are, whoever you're created by God to be on earth, you become that in heaven. I would have made a great princess or queen if my relationship with Charles had worked out. I was born for that. But heaven has awakened other desires in me and other parts and dimensions of me. I can do those things in heaven. I will cover that in the next question.

What I really love about heaven is that every individual can shine and be a star. Everyone can become the very best person that they can possibly be. They can live out that life in heaven and become everything that they always desired to be.

Even if they never desired to be something while still on earth, a desire that they might have never felt can awaken in their hearts in heaven. I just felt a hint of that on earth because time is consumed with trying to earn a living. Many people on earth are in survival mode. In heaven, you can fully explore who you are and do what your mind sets itself to do.

God is in control, and God understands our desires and what we're born to do. The Trinity will lead you toward what you're destined to do. You won't be stuck in a job in heaven, but you can actually go and study and learn to do other jobs. You can progress from what you thought was your last destiny to something else that is even more fulfilling and more exciting for you.

Once you have a job in heaven, it doesn't mean that's the last job that you will have. You can grow, explore, change direction, and do multiple things in heaven. That's a little bit about heaven. Mary explains what she likes in heaven in the book that Matthew wrote about her. For more about heaven from Michael Jackson, read Matthew's book, _Michael Jackson Speaks from Heaven: A Divine Revelation_. The saints in the book, _Great Cloud of Witnesses Speak_, talk about what they like in heaven. Some of Matthew's other books have plenty of descriptions of heaven as well. I hope you've enjoyed what I had to say about heaven.

Next, we'll talk about the job that I'm currently doing in heaven and how I'm spending my time right now.

Question 4:

What are you doing in heaven?

Initially, when I came to heaven, I was given a job similar to a princess, a queen, or a dignitary. I served with Mary Magdalene, and we did quite a few functions together. Just like the queen and the princes, Prince Harry, Prince William, and Prince Charles, they open government buildings and oversee ceremonies at all kinds of official functions in London and the United Kingdom.

You have heard me talk about how I love the fashion of heaven. You have heard me talk about studying fashion in heaven.

How many of you knew that I love fashion so much that I studied to become a fashion designer in heaven? How many of you knew that I have designed many clothes that people wear in heaven? Of course, when you're in heaven, everything is free.

Heaven is different because it's like an equalizer. People have come from earth who know who I am and who love me for who I am. Of course, some of them would like to have my fashions.

Different designs appeal to certain people, just like on earth when certain fashion designers come out with creations that everyone wants to wear. Some designers create fashion that's more suitable for everyday wear. Others design clothes that are appropriate to wear when you dress up to go out.

Different designers on earth appeal to different people, and the same is true for my designs. Some of my gowns are worn by people going to official functions in heaven while other gowns are worn by people who are going to smaller functions. I have a range of everyday clothes that people just wear out to restaurants. I have official evening wear. I even have a range of swimsuits for people to wear.

I have all different types of designs. Although I won't mention the name of the designer, I'm happy to say that some of my designs have found their way into the catalogues of some of the designers on earth. They have been inspired by my designs as thoughts about them came into their mind. I'm happy to say that I've seen actresses and wealthy women wearing a dress or a design of mine on earth. I can still turn heads on earth without people even knowing it, and that makes me smile.

Many of the songs and creations on earth were first designed in heaven by designers, architects, and other creative people. I have my own fashion label in heaven, and thousands and thousands of people wear my designs. I have a pretty good reputation there, not because I'm Princess Diana or Lady Diana but because I know fashion. For years while I was on earth, I wore the very best fashions and made certain fashion designers popular by wearing what they designed.

Of course, I was regularly on every cover of magazines all around the world with pictures of me in clothes from the world's best fashion designers. Now, I design my own creations, and I really have fun. I also visit people, and I have a small role in Matthew's life similar to a guardian angel. I'm sure that after this book is finished that the Lord Jesus will open up opportunities for me to visit other people and interact with them.

But at present, I spend a lot of my time in heaven in my own studio where I design clothes and certain fashions. I really enjoy myself. The people who come to my shop and pick clothes for themselves are very happy with what I'm making and with my designs. However, they don't have to come to my shop to see my designs because I have catalogues that feature my clothes. After they look through the catalogue, they come to my shop and choose what they want. Different from fashion designers on earth, I meet and interact with all my customers. It makes me really happy to go to a function and see a few people dressed in my designs and creations. I'm starting to understand how a fashion designer feels when someone wears their design and makes it popular.

Question 5:

What is Jesus like?

Have you ever had a man in your life like your grandfather or someone older than your father who was just full of love for you? As a child, you could climb up on his lap and pull on his beard, and he just loved it. He understands you and loves you and will do anything for you. He will play with you all day, will love you for who you are, and even be a little mysterious. He is full of love for you.

That's one way to explain Jesus. When you meet him, it's as if you've known him all of your life. There's this feeling of familiarity of being known, of being accepted. There's this childlike wonder that you have in his company. It's just like your grandfather or that older man, comfortable and lovely.

Jesus isn't full of rules. He isn't harsh. He isn't like many Christians that you meet. He isn't angry or upset and doesn't dictate all of these rules to you. He's totally relatable. He's so full of love. You can look into his eyes and just melt. He's the husband I was looking for. He really is.

Many of you know a lot more about my life than Matthew knows. On earth, I was searching for Jesus all the time. I was looking for a love that I found in Jesus' eyes. Jesus looks at you and knows you completely. You become undone.

Have you ever wanted to talk to someone for a hundred hours so that they see you and understand you? Matthew realizes that authors have a lot to say. Essentially, they're basically asking in their books, "Can you see me? Please understand me."

Well, you live in a really harsh world where people don't have the time or the energy to invest in getting to know each other. We spend our lives trying to connect with a person and hoping that they understand and love us for who we are. Jesus loves you for who you are. He seeks you out.

I've never been so completely understood or taken by anyone as by the way Jesus looks at me. He lavishes his love upon me. When you look into Jesus' eyes and you feel his love for you, you're ruined; you're ruined and just undone when he speaks to you. You're completely exposed, and you're ruined for any other man. No man on earth can compete with Jesus. No one.

I've met the apostles. I've met the popular people in the Bible. I've met Paul, Peter, and John, the disciple. I've met the heroes of the Bible.

None of them compared to Jesus. People like Moses are very touching. The Apostle John is really lovely. James, Jesus' brother, has a lot of similarities to Jesus, but he's not Jesus.

Other men in heaven are beautiful, but no one can hold a candle to Jesus. No one can compete with the love that he has for you. No one. There's no one. I'm ruined.

Of course, there's no marriage in heaven. There isn't any other man for me. Jesus is my sweetheart and is really the epitome of manhood. He's solid, strong with tremendous biceps, and full of authority. He can trample down kings.

He's physically strong and capable. He's a man's man. Even so, he's gentle as a dove, gentle as a lamb. He's so sweet and romantic.

To be held in Jesus' arms, in the crook of his neck, is just another experience. To have Jesus hold you, to have him hold your hand, kiss you on the cheek, and whisper in your ear is just so romantic. It's amazing and so lovely.

Jesus is everything to me. I don't know if I've overstated it. I don't think you could ever overstate Jesus. I don't think you could ever say too much about him. I don't think it's possible to exaggerate how good he is because there are no exaggerations.

He's the beginning and the end. He's the Creator of the universe. He is all-powerful, all-knowing, and all-loving. He knows everything. He is everything.

He is everywhere. He is amazing. You should get to know him. I'm so fortunate that I knew him and that I had a relationship with him before I died.

I'm so fortunate that I'm in heaven. He's beautiful. You should get to know him. I'm not talking about the Jesus that some Christians might preach but the Jesus who's in the Gospels, the Jesus that's in the books of Matthew, Mark, Luke, and John. Read for yourself about this Jesus and read what he taught.

Read what he taught in Matthew, Mark, Luke, and John. Matthew's written a book called *The Parables of Jesus Made Simple: Updated and Expanded Edition*. Read that book. Understand the teachings of Jesus. Of course, you can read books about a person. You can read a book about President Trump, or you can actually meet the man. You can read a book about Jesus. You can read Matthew, Mark, Luke, and John that tell of Jesus and his life. The Gospels are remarkable. You find a solid understanding of Jesus when you know what he taught in Matthew's book about the parables. You can get a glimpse into some of the concepts that Jesus was talking about.

Many people on earth have little understanding of Jesus. Sadly, even some of the people who run churches have little understanding of who Jesus is, but when you meet Jesus in heaven, when he looks into your eyes, when he holds you in his gaze, when he puts his hands out and holds your face and speaks to you, you're forever undone. You're touched beyond comprehension and powerfully affected.

There's no end to Jesus. When you look into his eyes, you can see eternity. You can look into the eyes of Jesus and see the future of the earth and of all mankind. You can look into the eyes of Jesus and see the world as John Lennon described it in the song, "Imagine." You can see the very creation of earth and of time. In Jesus, you can see the love and the compassion of God our Father.

You can watch Jesus as he interacts with the children as they run around him and jump up. He picks them up, skips rope with them, and wrestles with them. He climbs over playground equipment with them. He goes to amusement parks and slides down slides and rides roller coasters with them.

Children follow him. He's like the Pied Piper in the story. The children of heaven just love Jesus, and he has so much time for them. When you watch Jesus with the children, it's hard not to cry with tears welling up in your eyes because you see the attention he pays to just one child and the time that he spends with that child. You see that he is with a group of children, and he'll gather them all together and tell them a fascinating story. If you listen to the story, it's amazing.

Jesus is very good at sharing his past. He's very open and transparent. I think that Matthew is the same if you read many of his books. Jesus will often share with children about his life as a child and what he experienced as he was growing up. He'll take them back two thousand years when he was on earth and how he struggled to become the promised Messiah despite the rejection of the people.

Jesus is amazing. It's hard to explain it in words because he is immortal. It's hard to define something that's so wide with so much width and so much breadth. He's so high. There's no one higher, lower, and no one wider. You know, you can fit the whole universe inside Jesus. Jesus is as big as the universe. He really is the Savior of my soul.

One thing I regret is not pursuing him with passion when I was on earth. If you want to learn from what I have to say today, if you really want to listen to something in this book of mine, get to know Jesus.

Matthew has a book called _7 Keys to Intimacy with Jesus._ Buy that book. Put the information in that book into practice. Come to know Jesus for who he is. Do yourself a favor and get to know him. He really is the way, the truth, and the life. He really is the answer to life. Your life in heaven will be a whole lot better, richer, and more fulfilling if you already know Jesus before you get to heaven. Of course, you know him best when you're in heaven.

To walk with him, talk with him, laugh with him, and get carried away with the emotions of life with him in heaven is just something that has to be experienced. It can't be explained. I find that even my words are falling short. It's like trying to explain the sound of a symphony with words. It's so hard to capture and define. He's so beautiful, amazing, and exquisite. He really is the answer to your life and to everything you want to know. I hope that you come to know Jesus and love him for who he is. I hope that you come to know him before you die.

Question 6:

What is your message for your admirers?

First of all, I want to say that I love you. I love you with a love that can't be contained. It can't be described or captured. So many of you will buy this book and will want it when it's free. Well, you bought this book because you loved me. When I was alive, you would have loved me for who I was, who I represented, and the kind of woman that I was then.

Many of you are loyal, loving, and beautiful, and I love you for that. But I'm no one compared to Jesus. I'm not the most popular darling of heaven. Mary Magdalene captures the heart of heaven. She is sort of the Princess Diana of heaven. She's amazing, and she holds that position well. I'm just an ordinary, young girl who married a prince one day. I want to tell you that whatever you do, make sure that you are saved so that you can go to heaven.

You might have come across certain Christians who seem bombastic, rude, offensive, and who act nothing like Christ. However, you've heard what I've said about Jesus. That isn't Jesus. He is real and beautiful. I know that you can get to know him.

I encourage you all to pray to Jesus. Ask him to be a part of your life. At the end of this book, I include a prayer that you can pray to invite Jesus into your life. I really encourage you to pray this prayer. If you don't identify as a Christian, ask Jesus to come into your life.

I want to encourage Christians to rededicate their lives to Jesus today. Purchase the book, *7 Keys to Intimacy with Jesus,* and come to know him in such a way that you could also talk with saints. No matter your relationship with the Lord, I encourage you to buy *Great Cloud of Witnesses Speak* and listen to nineteen saints of the Bible speak about what life is like and what they suggest you do as a believer in Christ.

I also encourage you to read *Mary Magdalene Speaks from Heaven: A Divine Revelation,* due out in September 2017, or *Michael Jackson Speaks from Heaven: A Divine Revelation*. Read the four books I just mentioned and get to know Jesus.

Pursue Jesus if you're not a Christian. If you admire me, become an admirer of Jesus. Invest your time in him. Read the Gospels of Matthew, Mark, Luke, and John found in the New Testament. Get to know Jesus. Read Matthew's book, *The Parables of Jesus Made Simple: Updated and Expanded Edition*. It's not too complex, and you can understand what Jesus taught. Even if you're a Christian, come to know what Jesus taught in that book.

If you want to know more about God the Father, read *Conversations with God: Book 1* and *Conversations with God: Book 2*. Read some of the things that God discussed with Matthew as they spoke together. If you want to know a little more about Jesus, read *Finding Intimacy with Jesus Made Simple* or *Jesus Speaking Today*.

All of these books are resources that Matthew directs people to so that they can find out more about Jesus. Jesus really is the answer. He really is the person that you should pursue. No one knows him as much as they could know him. You can never reach the stage where you know too much about Jesus.

You might want to avoid anyone who thinks they know too much about Jesus or a lot about him. Many people in this world think they have a lot of answers and assume that they know everything. Matthew has a solid relationship with Jesus, but there's so much more. I encourage you, if you admire me, come to know someone who's so much better than me. Get to know the saints in *Great Cloud of Witnesses Speak.* Get to know what they say about life and the Christian faith. Realize that it's important to do what they say in this generation. Read and understand the faith that they had in God and their relationship with him.

If you're struggling as a Christian and you don't know your purpose in life, perhaps you can read *Finding Your Purpose in Christ* by Matthew. If you love me, come to know Jesus and develop your relationship with him. Ask him, "Can you talk to me? Can he send me down to talk to you? Can you have a conversation with me?"

When you can speak with Jesus and communicate with the Holy Spirit and when your spiritual senses are in tune so that you can hear spiritually, you'll be able to speak to me. You can dialogue with me and have a conversation with me. I love you, and the best thing I can do for all of you who love me is to direct you all to Jesus through the resources I have mentioned.

Question 7:

What is your message for Christians?

One of the meanings for the word "Christian" is little Christ. This essentially means that you are a representation of Christ on earth.

Now, if you really look at yourself and do any self-examination, many of you would realize that you don't really reflect Jesus Christ in your actions and your words. Others might be Christ-like in some respects. Many Christians do reflect Christ, but so many more don't reflect him.

One way to get to know Jesus Christ is to understand his teachings and what he had to say. John 14:21 says, "He who has My commandments and keeps them, it is he who loves Me. And he who loves Me will be loved by My Father, and I will love him and manifest Myself to him."

Did you know that a person only loves me when they obey my commands? Did you know that they only love Jesus when they obey his commands? Many Christians have no idea that Jesus had fifty commands. Matthew repeats this over and over in his books. Here is the link to that article on the fifty commands of Jesus. Click here for the link if you're reading an e-book. If you're reading a paperback, search Google for the fifty commands of Jesus.

As a Christian, you need to not only understand Jesus by reading the Gospels but understand and practice what he taught. Jesus said in Matthew 15:8, "These people . . . honor Me with their lips, but their heart is far from me." Jesus said in Matthew 7:22-23, "Many people will say to Me in that day, 'Lord, Lord . . . .' and I will declare to them, 'I never knew you; depart from me . . . .'"

Jesus is a loving, beautiful person, but he has a sober side to him. He has a heart of justice, and the people in the world really deserve to meet him through you.

Not many people in the world actually have a vision of Jesus and can meet him before they become a Christian. The people of the world are really depending on you to demonstrate Jesus to them. They're counting on you to be such a beautiful person that you attract them to the very nature and the very person of Jesus.

It's one thing to call yourself a Christian, and many people do call themselves a Christian. However, it's quite another thing to be a born-again Christian, to accept Jesus into your life, and accept Jesus as your Lord and Savior, someone who rules your life.

Many born-again Christians are in the world, but a Christian moves to another level when he or she knows what Jesus taught and practices those things. 1 John 2:6 says, "He who says he abides in Him ought himself also to walk just as He walked." John was saying here that a person who has a close and abiding relationship with Jesus must behave and act like Jesus.

The Apostle Paul says in 1 Corinthians 11:1, "Imitate me as I imitate Christ." How many people imitate Christ? How many people are walking around as a practical demonstration of Jesus? This is what the world needs from you.

The world needs you to be Jesus and to imitate him. The world needs to meet Jesus in you. The world is perishing. People are dying every day without the saving knowledge of Jesus Christ.

People are being led astray. They do not know Jesus. Even I would have loved to have known someone who knew Jesus as well as Matthew, for instance. Even I could have benefitted from having a close relationship with someone who was intimately in relationship with Jesus.

I encourage you to buy these books, which are all 99 cents. Buy *The Parables of Jesus Made Simple: Updated and Expanded Edition*. Get the book, *Finding Intimacy with Jesus Made Simple*. Get the book, *Jesus Speaking Today*.

Read these books and connect with them. Buy the book, *7 Keys to Intimacy with Jesus,* and put those keys into practice. Put the seven steps to getting to know Jesus into practice. Don't just read the book, apply it.

The Holy Spirit told Matthew a number of years ago that wisdom is the proper application of knowledge. A lot of knowledge is in the world, but very few people walk in wisdom. The Christian faith isn't about knowing what Jesus taught but about applying and obeying what he taught.

The world seriously needs Christians who are obeying Jesus. The world is crying out for the Son of God to be manifested on earth and for people to not only confess Jesus Christ and believe in him but to practice what Jesus Christ taught and to be as he is to this world. Are you going to be a Christian, or are you going to be Jesus?

Question 8:

What is your message to your loved ones?

I cannot promise that this will ever reach my loved ones. Someone who reads this book might have to send it on and notify them about it. However, it's important for you to read and to hear what I would say to my loved ones.

I feel that this chapter is an integral part of this book. One of the questions Matthew asked and one of the reasons why I'm going to answer it is because it's important for you, the reader, to know that when you go to heaven, things change.

The first person that I want to speak to is Prince Charles, my former husband. I want you to know that I love you. I want you to know that you really have some wonderful qualities that I admire. I still have a deep love in my heart for you. I encourage you to pursue Jesus and to seek out the true desire of the world, the true Master, the true Master-Teacher, the true Anointed One.

So many distractions, false positions, and false leaders are in the world. You can run after these and try to impress so many people of authority in the world. There's only one entity in the world that you need to impress and that's Jesus and his Father God. I pray that your heart would be softened and that you would come to know Jesus as I know him now.

I have a message for Camilla. I send my love and praise for your marriage. I pray quite often for the happiness of you and

Charles. I love you both, and I really respect you for coming alongside Charles and being his wife and standing by him through all of his life, his trials, and his struggles. God bless you.

I have a message for the Queen. I love you, Elizabeth. I always deeply admired you. I had tremendous respect for you though I admit that my attitude and my behavior didn't always respect your office. I failed you in many ways. That was both due to my innocence and my lack of understanding protocol and also due to deliberate rebellion and refusal to come under your authority and your direction.

I repent and apologize publicly to you for disrespecting your office and disrespecting you as a person. I look forward to hugging you, getting to know you, and loving you when you come to heaven shortly. I look forward to building a lifetime with you in paradise with Jesus. I look forward to serving with you and even dressing you in some of my fashions. It would be an honor to dress you.

I have a message for my son, William. I admire you greatly. Mothers always have a special place in their heart for their sons. As my first-born, you have given me much happiness; you've given me much latitude when it comes to my ability to respect you.

You're so straightforward, honest, and sincere with much integrity. You're a man of great morals and leadership skills. I wish you well in your life and in your future as you possibly become the future King of England.

I send my love to your lovely wife, Kate, and to your children. I send my blessings. Kate is like sunshine to the dawn. She's like the sunrise on the new day, and it becomes sunset when she sets like the sun. She is an inspiration to you, William, and I love her very much and deeply respect her and your children.

Last but not least, I send my love to Harry. I really love the mysterious ways that you have and your unbridled energy. You have a zest for life. I'm glad that you made it through your depression. I really love your current girlfriend. I know that you are a survivor.

You're a little bit like me. You're a survivor. Cats always land on their feet no matter what distance you drop them from the ground. You will always land on your feet. I'm very proud of you and hopeful for your future. I certainly pray for you.

All of these people—Charles, Camilla, Queen Elizabeth, William, Harry, and Kate—I love you so dearly, and I hope that someone might pass this book onto you so that you can read my message. The readers of this book are greatly encouraged that I had the opportunity to express and share my heart and to practically demonstrate the change that heaven has made on my attitudes and on how I behaved.

Also, before I go, I want to publicly apologize to Camilla for my behavior regarding Charles. I want to publicly apologize to Charles for my behavior and the way that I disrespected you. I pray that one day in eternity, when we all are in heaven, that everything will be resolved, and we can be great friends then.

Question 9:

What are your final words?

My parting words to you are to learn to love. I believe that John shares the secret of life when he says in 1 John 4:8, "God is love." Everything that relates to love is an expression of God within us. Without God in the universe, you don't have love. I encourage every one of you to pray the prayer at the end of this book and invite Jesus into your life. I encourage all of you to pursue an intimate relationship with Jesus. For further help, I've listed several of Mathew's books as resources.

If you're a Christian who wants to read more about the concept of grace, buy *Destined to Reign* by Joseph Prince. This book will free you up and open your understanding of the God of love and help you understand the way that he demonstrates his love on earth. I am really pleased to be with you. Some audio books about me will last more than ten hours. This audio book will last about two hours.

Many people might wonder what I had to say about the people that were part of my life on earth. Many people probably hoped to hear my opinions about my life on earth. People are probably wondering and still questioning if my death was an accident or if it was actually planned.

The answer is innocent. The plan was not for me to be killed. Some people do assume that. However, Michael Jackson's death was planned.

In my case, it was an accident, yet I can understand that people who hear me might not be convinced by these words. God is the

God of forgiveness. If I've learned anything in heaven, I've learned to forgive. I have nothing but love for every person on earth.

My greatest desire is that everyone comes to a saving knowledge of Jesus Christ. I'm not saying that Christianity has all the answers. I don't think you can misread me in that respect. However, I am saying that Jesus Christ is the most beautiful man in the universe.

It's worth your time to pursue him and to live a life worthy of him. Center your life on him. He really is the way, the truth, and the life. He really is the way to leave your old life behind; he carries the truth of life, and he gives your life meaning.

If you're Christian, I suggest that you read the book, _Finding Your Purpose in Christ_. If you want to influence others as a Christian, I suggest that you read _Influencing Your World for Christ_. If you want to know more about Jesus, I suggest that you read _Finding Intimacy with Jesus Made Simple_.

I have so many things that I could tell you and much more that I could continue to say, but the book has to end at some point. Perhaps I can come down and answer more questions in the future in a second book.

If I was going to spend a couple of hours on earth, I wanted to spend my time talking about the most important things to me and the most important things to Christ. I really encourage you to seek out the person of Jesus Christ, the Son of God. Put your faith in him, draw close to him, and pursue him with everything that you have. Life might not get easier. It's a fallacy that the Christian life is an easy life. The Christian life is hard, but you'll be rewarded in the end.

It would be great to see all of the readers of this book. I'm watching every one of you who is reading this book. I'm talking to you.

It's important that I see you in heaven with me. I'll greet you when you arrive. Every one of you who reads this book and who makes a decision to follow Jesus will be greeted by me, spend time with me, and have a lovely conversation with me. I look forward to seeing you in heaven.

If you want to meet me, spend time with me, or sit down and get to know me, do yourself a favor and pray the prayer at the end of this book. Accept Jesus into your life. Try to live a life that is worthy of him so that one day, you can go to heaven and meet Jesus, this man that has ravished my soul. Get to know me.

It's been fun being here. I'm going to continue to visit Mathew and to be part of his life. I look forward to meeting you, whether it be on earth or in heaven.

Closing thoughts

I have come to know Diana fairly well in a few visits. She seems to like me. It is her wish and mine that the readers of this book come to accept Jesus as their Savior. I therefore put this prayer here for you to pray when you are ready to do so.

If you are not a Christian and you want to commit your life to Jesus and become a Christian, simply pray this prayer with faith.

Dear God,

Please lead me to know more about Jesus and teach me how to be a Christian. I accept that I am a sinner. I ask that you forgive my sins and that you allow me to become a follower of Jesus. I know that Jesus died to save me. I thank Jesus for his sacrifice on the cross, and I give my life to you. Please send the Holy Spirit to come and dwell within me. Give me your peace and assurance that I am now a Christian.

In Jesus' Name I ask, Amen.

If you prayed that prayer, I encourage you to contact a Christian that you know and let them know that you prayed a prayer to become a Christian. Ask them how you can learn more about the Christian faith and ask them to help you. Please contact me at survivors.sanctuary@gmail.com and tell me about your decision as well.

I'd love to hear from you

One of the ways that you can bless me as a writer is by writing an honest and candid review of my book on Amazon. I always read the reviews of my books, and I would love to hear what you have to say about this one.

Before I buy a book, I read the reviews first. You can make an informed decision about a book when you have read enough honest reviews from readers. One way to help me sell this book and to give me positive feedback is by writing a review for me. It doesn't cost you a thing but helps me and the future readers of this book enormously.

If you would like to sow money into a portion of a book or even into an entire book, please visit my website and ask me what projects I am working on.

To read my blog, request a life-coaching session, request your own personal prophecy, request a visit to heaven, or to receive a personal message from your angel, or any other of the services I offer, you can also visit my website at http://personal-prophecy-today.com All of the funds raised through my ministry website will go toward the books that I write and self-publish. Feel free to sow money into my book-publishing ministry as the Holy Spirit leads you.

To write to me about this book or to share any other thoughts, please feel free to contact me at my personal email address at survivors.sanctuary@gmail.com

You can also friend request me on Facebook at Matthew Robert Payne. Please send me a message if we have no friends in common as a lot of scammers now send me friend requests.

You can also do me a huge favor and share this book on Facebook as a recommended book to read. This will help me and other readers.

Other Books by Matthew Robert Payne

The Prophetic Supernatural Experience

Prophetic Evangelism Made Simple

Your Identity in Christ

His Redeeming Love- A Memoir

Writing and Self-Publishing Christian Nonfiction

Coping with your Pain and Suffering

Living for Eternity

Jesus Speaking Today

Great Cloud of Witnesses Speak

My Radical Encounters with Angels

Finding Intimacy with Jesus Made Simple

My Radical Encounters with Angels- Book Two

A Beginner's Guide to the Prophetic

Michael Jackson Speaks from Heaven

7 Keys to Intimacy with Jesus

Conversations with God: Book 1

Optimistic Visions of Revelation

Conversations with God: Book 2

Finding Your Purpose in Christ

Influencing your World for Christ: Practical Everyday Evangelism

Deep Calls unto Deep: Answering Questions on the Prophetic

My Visits to the Galactic Council of Heaven

The Parables of Jesus Made Simple: Updated and Expanded Edition

Great Cloud of Witnesses Speak: Old and New

Walking under an Open Heaven

A Message from My Angel Book 1

Interviews with the Two Witnesses: Enoch and Elijah Speak

Gaining Freedom from Sex Addictions: Breaking Free of Pornography and Prostitutes

Mary Magdalene Speaks from Heaven: A Divine Revelation

You can find my published books on my Amazon author page here: http://tinyurl.com/jq3h893

Upcoming books

A Message from My Angel: Book 2

How to Hear God's Voice: Keys to Conversational Two-Way Prayer

About Matthew Robert Payne

Matthew was raised in a Baptist church and was led to the Lord at the tender age of eight. He has experienced some pain and darkness in his life, which has given him a deep compassion and love for all people.

Today, he runs a Facebook group called "Open Heavens and Intimacy with Jesus." Matthew has a commission from the Lord to train up prophets and to mentor others in the Christian faith. He does this through his Facebook posts and by writing relevant books on the Christian faith.

God has commissioned him to write at least fifty books in his life, and he spends his days writing and earning the money to self-publish. You can support him by donating money at http://personal-prophecy-today.com or by requesting any of his other services available through his ministry website.

It is Matthew's prayer that this book has blessed you, and he hopes it will lead you into a deeper and more intimate relationship with God.

www.ingramcontent.com/pod-product-compliance
Lightning Source LLC
Chambersburg PA
CBHW072159060526
44654CB00046B/1361